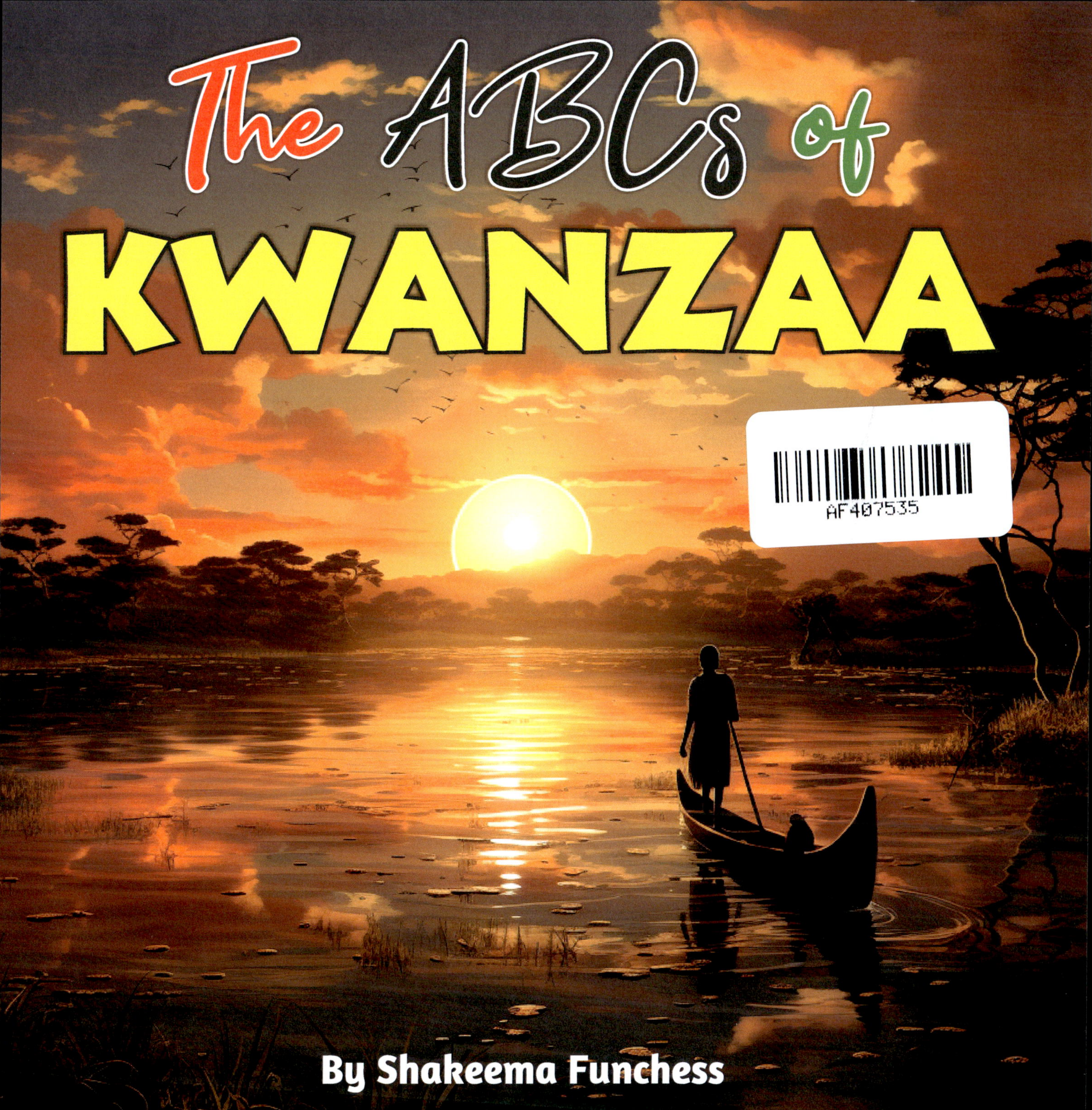

The ABCs of
KWANZAA
By Shakeema Funchess

Illustrations by AI

This Books Belongs To:

____

How do we say it?

Kwanzaa (KWAN-za) comes from the Swahili word meaning first fruits.

Nguzo Saba (n-Gu-zo SAH-bah) refers to the seven principles Kwanzaa is based upon.

Umoja (oo-MO-jah) the first principle celebrated on the first day means unity.

Kujichagulia (koo-jee-chah-GOO-lee-ah) the second principle celebrated on the second day means self-determination.

Ujima (oo-JEE-mah) the third principle celebrated on the third day means collective work and responsibility.

Ujamaa (oo-jah-MAH-ah) the fourth principle celebrated on the fourth day means cooperative economics.

Nia (NEE-ah) the fifth principle celebrated on the fifth day means purpose.

Kuumba (koo-OOM-bah) the sixth principle celebrated on the sixth day means creativity.

Imani (ee-MAH-nee) the seventh principle celebrated on the last day of Kwanzaa means faith.

Habari gani? (Ha-ba-ri ga-ni) is the question asked at the start of every Kwanzaa celebration or when greeting each other. It is Swahili for, "What is the news?". The response is the Nguzo Saba (principle) for that day.

Harambee! (hah-RAHM-beh) is the call of unity shouted at the end of each night's celebration means "Let's pull together!".

A is for Africa, where roots took hold,
Kwanzaa's origins, where stories unfold.
Dr. Maulana Karenga, a scholar and sage,
Brought forth this celebration on history's stage.

B is for Black, the color of unity,
In Kwanzaa's flag, it represents our community.

C is for candles, seven in all,
Lit on Kinara, three red, one black,
three green to answer Kwanzaa's call.
Each day's a principle, a lesson to learn,
Unity, purpose, and love, something we all can earn.

D is for drumming, the heartbeat of soul,
With rhythms and melodies, our spirits become whole.
In Kwanzaa's circle, we dance and we sing,
As we honor our heritage and let our hearts swing.

E is for elders, wise and dear,
Their wisdom and guidance, we hold them near.
They pass down traditions and stories of old,
Keeping Kwanzaa's spirit alive and bold.

F is for family, the foundation we build,
Through love and support, our spirits are fulfilled.
Kwanzaa's about kinship, togetherness, and care,
With bonds that are strong, and hearts that are rare.

G is for gifts, not bought from a store,
But meaningful tokens, from the heart to the core.
Handmade or handwritten, they speak of our love,
A symbol of blessings sent from above.

H is for harvest, the bounty we share,
Fruits of our labor, a symbol so fair.
In unity, we gather, and feasting we find,
The fruits of our efforts, both body and mind.

I is for identity, who we truly are,
Kwanzaa reminds us, we are a shining star.
African and proud, our heritage we embrace,
A unique and rich culture, a beautiful space.

J is for joy, the laughter we bring,
During Kwanzaa's festivities, we all sing.
With smiles on our faces, and hearts full of cheer,
We celebrate the season; with those we hold dear.

K is for Kwanzaa, our cultural delight,
A seven-day festival, shining so bright.
It's a time to remember, a time to reflect,
On principles and values, we should never neglect.

L is for love, the most potent of all,
In Kwanzaa's warm embrace, we stand tall.
With love in our hearts, and love in our deeds,
We sow the seeds of unity, meeting all our needs.

M is for mindfulness, a tranquil retreat,
Reflecting on life, finding balance so sweet.
In silence, we discover strength, our inner core,
Kwanzaa's wisdom guides us, all year we'll explore.

N is for Nguzo Saba, the seven principles we hold,
Umoja, Kujichagulia, Ujima, and so we're told,
Ujamaa, Nia, Kuumba, and Imani's our guide,
They lead us on the path of Kwanzaa's pride.

O is for origin, Africa's our root,
Kwanzaa reminds us of our heritage, we are the fruit.
From Egypt to Mali, and the Nile's grand flow,
Our ancestral ties, no matter where we live still show.

P is for purpose, the drive deep within,
Kwanzaa inspires us to know where to begin.
With goals and intentions, we're guided each day,
To make the world better, in every single way.

Q is for questions, the wisdom we seek,
Kwanzaa's a journey, a path so deep.
We ask and we learn, from elders and youth,
With knowledge and understanding, we find our truth.

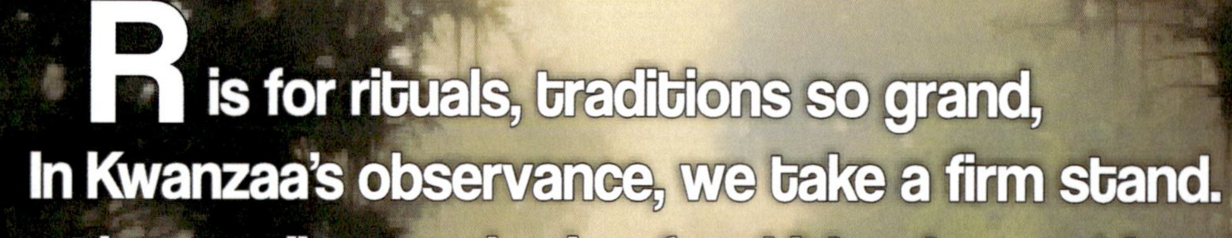

R is for rituals, traditions so grand,
In Kwanzaa's observance, we take a firm stand.
From lighting the candles to sharing food it's a happy time full of cheer,
Each act holds meaning, a source for us to gather and be near.

S is for symbols, like the Kinara's light,
The red, black, and green, in our Kwanzaa night.
The mazao and zawadi, the symbols so dear,
In each one, a message, loud and clear.

T is for togetherness, unity's grace,
In Kwanzaa's embrace, we find our place.
As a family and community, we stand side by side,
Facing life's challenges with unwavering pride.

U is for Uplift, our hearts take flight,
Kwanzaa's spirit lifts us to new heights.
Together we rise, with purpose in view,
In Kwanzaa's embrace, dreams we pursue.

V is for values, we hold in our heart,
Kwanzaa instills them, right from the start.
Respect and responsibility, we always uphold,
With Kwanzaa's teachings, our lives are gold.

W is for wisdom, from the past we gain,
In Kwanzaa's reflection, we break every chain.
The elders' stories, their lessons we peep,
Guide us on our journey, as we boldly leap.

X is for exploring, the adventures we chase,
With Kwanzaa's principles, we find our place.
The legacy we leave, for generations to come,
A brighter tomorrow, for everyone.

Y is for you and me, together we strive,
In Kwanzaa's spirit, our hearts come alive.
With love, hope, and purpose, we stand hand in hand,
Celebrating Kwanzaa, across the land.

Z is for zeal, the passion we share,
For Kwanzaa's traditions, we show that we care.
From A to Z, the story is told,
Kwanzaa's legacy, forever enfolded.

Additional Kwanzaa words:

Mazao (mah-ZAH-oh) is the bowl of fruit and vegetables in the Kwanzaa display.

Zawadi (zah-WAH-dee) means gifts, they are exchanged throughout Kwanzaa.

Muhinid (moo-HEEN-dee) are the ears of corn in the Kwanzaa display. There is one placed for each child in the family.

Mkeka (em-KEH-kah) is the straw mat centerpiece in a Kwanzaa display.

Kikombe cha umoja (kee-KOHM-bee chah oo-MOH-jah) means unity cup. It sits in the Kwanzaa display and during the day's celebration the family will share a drink from it.

Kinara (kee-NAH-rah) is the candle holder in the center of the Kwanzaa display.

Mishumaa saba (mee-shoo-MAH-ah SAH-ba) are the seven candles of the kinara that represent the Nguzo Saba of Kwanzaa.

Karamu (kah-RAH-moo) is the big feast celebrated on the sixth day of Kwanzaa (December 31st).

What are the colors of Kwanzaa?

Red represents the struggle of the African ancestors. Black represents the unified African/African American people. Green represents the fertile lands of Africa and the hope for all its children no matter where they live.

History of Kwanzaa

Kwanzaa, the first African American holiday, was created by Dr. Maulana Karenga in 1966. The holiday is designed to help African Americans reconnect with their African heritage. The holiday is observed yearly from December 26th to January 1st. The holiday can be celebrated alongside other holidays such as Hanukkah, Christmas, or New Year's.

The Seven Principles of Kwanzaa each have their own dedicated day of celebration. The Seven Principles of Kwanzaa were originally called the Seven Principles of Blackness. During celebration the Kikombe cha Umoja (Unity cup) is filled with water, grape juice or wine. After taking a sip the cup is raised and Harambee (Let's pull together) is shouted. During the Kwanzaa celebrations music is played and the African pledge can be read.

Other Titles by the Author You May Like:
A Journey Through Black History
The ABCs of Black History
The ABCs of Healthcare: A Journey Through Health and Healing
The ABCs of Hip Hop: 50 Years of Black Excellence
The ABCs of Juneteenth
ABCs of the NBA
ABCs of the WNBA
The Adventures of Renata and Linus
The Adventures of Sanjay and Semaj
Double Rainbow: Sanjay has Two Moms
Julian's Jam: Strings of Joy
Kaya's Story: Exploring Indigenous Culture
Logan the Little Learner: First Day of Daycare
Me Llamo Xiomara: A Tale of Hispanic Heritage and Identity
Nastasia's March: An Army of Hope
Night, Night Safari: Farewell Fun with Furry Friends
Parading with Pride: Rediscovering the Pinkster Festival
Paws and Pumpkins: A Halloween Tale
Sea Safari: Amara and Bemba's Underwater Encounters
SheShe's Soulful Kitchen: Cooking with Grandma
The Three Sisters and the Fair Share: Learning About Equality and Equity